39 Awesome 1-1 ESL Activities:

For Teenagers and Adults

Jackie Bolen +

Jennifer Booker Smith

Copyright 2015 by Jackie Bolen + Jennifer Booker Smith

All rights reserved. No part of this publication may be reproduced, distributed, or transmitted in any form or by any means, including photocopying, recording or other electronic or mechanical means without the prior written permission of the publisher, except in the case of brief quotations in critical reviews and certain other noncommercial uses permitted by copyright law. For permission requests, write to the publisher/author at the address below.

Jackie Bolen: jb.business.online@gmail.com

Table of Contents

About the Author: Jackie Bolen..4
About the Author: Jennifer Booker Smith..5
How to Use this Book..6
39 Awesome 1-1 ESL Activities..7
    120-90-60 Fluency Activity..7
    20 Questions..8
    2 Truths and a Lie..10
    Agony Aunt..11
    Boggle..14
    Brochure Scanning...15
    Chapter Response...17
    Character Problems and Solutions...18
    Conversation Starters...19
    Cosmo Quiz..20
    Deserted Island...21
    Dictogloss...22
    English Central...23
    Find the Reference...24
    Flyer Time..25
    Fortunately, Unfortunately/Luckily, Unluckily...26
    If I Had a Million Dollars..27
    Infographic Presentation..28
    Is that Sentence Correct?...30
    Just a Minute..31
    Just Fill in This Form, Please..32
    Mystery Case Files..33
    New Language Pile Up..34
    Proofreading/Editing..35
    Real House Hunters...36
    Real Life Role Play...37
    Scaffolded Reading Online..38

Sentence Substitution Ladder..39
Story Timeline..41
Tell Me More..42
Test Prep: Describing a Photo 43
Test Prep: Reading Aloud Fluently 44
Test Prep Speaking Activity: 5Ws and H...45
Test Prep: Speaking to Essay Writing..47
Text Me!..48
Where Are They Now?..49
Who do you Want at Your Party?..50
Word of the Day 51
Would You Rather...51
Before You Go..53

About the Author: Jackie Bolen

I've been teaching English in South Korea for a decade to every level and type of student and I've taught every age from kindergarten kids to adults. Most of my time has centered around teaching at two universities: five years at a science and engineering school out in the rice paddies of Chungcheongnam-Do, and four years at a major university in Busan where I now teach high level classes for students majoring in English. In my spare time, you can usually find me outside surfing, biking, hiking or on the hunt for the most delicious kimchi I can find.

In case you were wondering what my academic qualifications are, I hold a Master of Arts in Psychology. During my time in Korea I've successfully completed both the Cambridge CELTA and DELTA certification programs. With the combination of almost ten years teaching ESL/EFL learners of all ages and levels, and the more formal teaching qualifications I've obtained, I have a solid foundation on which to offer teaching advice. I truly hope that you find this book useful and would love it if you sent me an email with any questions or feedback that you might have (jb.business.online@gmail.com).

More From Jackie Bolen

If you like 39 Awesome 1-1 ESL Activities: For Teenagers and Adults, please leave a review over on Amazon and don't forget to check out our other books at the same time:

39 ESL Icebreakers: For Teenagers and Adults: It will get your semester started off on the right foot by helping the students get to know each other, and you.

39 No-Prep/Low-Prep ESL Speaking Activities: For Teenagers and Adults. Check out this book if you need some new ideas for your conversation classes.

101 Activities and Resources for Teaching English Online: Have better online ESL classes with these games, activities, and teaching tips.

Jackie Bolen Around the Internet

ESL Speaking (www.eslspeaking.org)

Jackie Bolen (www.jackiebolen.com)

Twitter: @bolen_jackie

Email: jb.business.online@gmail.com

About the Author: Jennifer Booker Smith

I have a Master of Education in TESOL and have spent fifteen years teaching students of all ages in Korea, from two-year-old preschoolers barely out of diapers to businessmen and even a semester as a teacher trainer at an education university. However, my greatest love is the middle primary grades—I left a fairly cushy teacher trainer position to return to the elementary classroom. In that age group, I've taught all ability levels from false beginner to near-native returnees.

During my time in the classroom, I've created countless board and card games and other resources. In this book, you'll find some of the vocabulary activities that I have used successfully (I've tried plenty which weren't successful!) in a variety of settings; these are the ones I've used again and again because they actually work.

When I'm not teaching, like Jackie, you can often find me hiking. I've taken up running recently and will soon be running my third half marathon. Teaching takes up a lot more "free" time than non-teachers will ever realize, so it's important to recharge the batteries and being outside is my favorite way to do just that.

You can get in touch with me by emailing jenniferteacher@gmail.com. I'd love to hear from you and help you with your classes in any way that I can.

How to Use this Book

We think that teaching 1-on-1 classes is quite difficult! While teachers don't have the same classroom management issues that they would with a group of 30 or 40 students, 1-on-1 classes are demanding in different ways. The first difficulty is that the majority of the activities or games that teachers would normally use in a classroom setting don't work when it's just one teacher and one student. The other reason is that it's more demanding on the teacher because he/she is required to interact the entire time—unlike in a classroom setting where a teacher normally sets up an activity and lets students work with a partner or in small groups.

Despite these difficulties, it is indeed possible to have engaging, interesting and productive 1-on-1 classes that don't leave you exhausted. We're confident that through using these 39 activities, your classes will be varied, fun and useful, and your lesson planning will be made easy. Try them out and please let us know which ones worked for you, which ones didn't and/or any new ideas for 1-on-1 activities that you have. We always appreciate any feedback from our readers.

So, dig in and kick that 1-on-1 lesson planning into high-gear with 39 Awesome 1-1 ESL Activities: For Teenagers and Adults! The vast majority of your 1-on-1 teenage or adult students are highly-motivated, and ready for whatever challenges you can throw at them.

39 Awesome 1-1 ESL Activities

120-90-60 Fluency Activity

Skills: Speaking/Listening

Time: 10 minutes

Level: Intermediate to Advanced

Materials: None

If you want to help your student speak more quickly and fluently, this is the perfect ESL speaking activity. Give your student a topic that he/she knows a lot about. For example: good or bad points about his/her school, university, or hometown. Give 3-5 minutes to prepare depending on the student's level, but emphasize writing just one or two words for each point —rather than full sentences because it is a speaking activity and not a writing one. Afterward, instruct the student to give a speech and talk continuously for two minutes, while you listen. I use my phone as a stopwatch so that the student can see the clock count down.

Next, instruct the student to repeat the activity, except now he/she has to include ALL the same information as before, and this time, there will only be 90 seconds. Then, tell the student to do it one more time within 60 seconds. One way that you can help your student make the transition to less time is by providing 30 seconds between rounds to think about how to say something more concisely. He/she can go over the parts of the speech where he/she had to slow down for some reason and think about where they to use conjunctions.

You could give an example of something like this: "I like watching The Simpsons. It's funny. It's interesting. My mother, father, brother and I watch while we're eating dinner almost every night of the week," ---> "I like watching The Simpsons because it's funny and interesting. I watch with my family almost every night while eating dinner."

For lower-level students, you can adjust the times to make them shorter and easier because talking for two minutes can be quite difficult for a beginner.

Teaching Tips:

It can be really difficult to find good speaking activities that are focused on fluency instead of accuracy, but this is an excellent one and I use it often.

Something that you can remind your student of is that speech is more informal than written discourse, particularly in the areas of sentence length and connectors. When we write, words like "however," "although" and "moreover" are common, but in speech we mostly just use simple connectors like "and," "but" and "or." Also, in spoken discourse the length of an utterance is much shorter and we don't need to use complicated grammatical constructions.

Procedure:

1. Give your student a topic and some time to prepare a "speech."

2. The student recites the speech, talking for two minutes without stopping.

3. The student gives the speech again, this time in 90 seconds. He/she must include all the same information as before so speaking must be quick and concise.

4. The student gives the speech one more time, but in 60 seconds, and makes sure to include all the same information.

20 Questions

Skills: Speaking/Listening
Time: 10 minutes
Level: High-Beginner to Advanced
Materials: None

This is a "20 questions" style game based on whatever you're teaching)such as animals or jobs) that is particularly effective for working on yes/no question forms and also logical thinking. If you have a higher level student, this works well as a warm-up or icebreaker activity. You can leave it open and allow the student to choose any person, place or thing.

The teacher starts the game by thinking of a secret thing, and the student can ask the teacher yes/no questions. Keep track of how many questions the student asks. Incorrect answers count as a guess, too. If the student guesses the secret thing within 20 guesses, he/she is the winner. If it takes the student more than 20 guesses though, the teacher is the winner. You can switch roles and play again.

Teaching Tips:

This game is easily adaptable to make it much easier or much more difficult. To make it very difficult, just say that the secret word has to be a noun. If you want to make it less difficult, specify a person, place or thing. Finally, the easiest version is to choose a more specific category such as animals or jobs. If you choose the easiest version, you might want to reduce the number of questions from 20 down to 10. For absolute beginners, it's useful to write some example questions on a whiteboard or piece of paper for them to refer to throughout the activity.

This is one of those "absolutely nothing required in the way of preparation or materials" games that can be played with a variety of levels and class sizes (from 1-40). Keep it in your bag of tricks to pull out in case of emergency.

Procedure:

1. The teacher chooses a secret thing and the student asks a yes/no question. The teacher answers the question and puts one tick (checkmark) on the paper to keep track of the number of questions.

2. The student asks more questions and the game continues until the student either guesses the secret thing or reaches 20 questions/guesses. If the student guesses the secret thing within 20 turns, he/she is the winner. If the students reaches 20 questions without guessing the correct answer, the teacher is the winner.

3. Each guess also counts as one question. This prevents random guessing.

4. You can switch roles and play again.

2 Truths and a Lie

Skills: Writing/Listening/Speaking

Time: 10-15 minutes

Level: Intermediate to Advanced

Materials: None

2 Truths and a Lie is a good activity to practice "always, usually, sometimes, never" or "can, can't" and "I've." Both the student and the teacher write three sentences (separately), one of which is false. The student reads his/her three sentences first and the teacher asks some follow-up questions for 2-5 minutes with the goal of uncovering the false one. After the question time, the teacher can guess which one is false. The teacher and student switch roles and play again.

Teaching Tips:

This is a useful activity for practicing the speaking sub-skills of initiating a conversation and responding to something in a questioning way. For example, the student will have to say something like, "So you can make/play/do _____? I kind of don't believe you! Tell me _____," if you allow question time.

Emphasize that the student must pick things that are "big picture" ideas. The "bad" examples I give are things like birthdays, hospital he/she was born in, name of sister, etc. There is simply no way to verify this information through asking any sort of interesting questions. Better categories are things like hobbies, travel, part-time jobs, skills and abilities. I have a quick check of my student's sentences before the activity starts to catch any of the bad ones before we begin.

Procedure:

1. Both the student and the teacher write three sentences about themselves, one of which is

false.

2. The student reads his/her three sentence and the teacher can ask some follow-up questions, attempting to discover the false one.

3. The teacher guesses which one is false and finds out if the guess was correct.

4. The student and teacher switch roles and the game continues.

Agony Aunt

Skills: Listening/Speaking

Time: 15-20 minutes

Level: High-beginner to Advanced

Materials: Printed advice column questions and answers

This activity will get your student talking because everyone knows how to solve other people's problems! If the student is a bit more advanced, you can use actual advice columns. These can easily be found by searching on the Internet for "advice column" etc. The lower the students' level, the more you'll need to grade the language, or you can write your own advice column.

I've done several variations of this activity and it has always been a hit. I begin with an introduction that shows a few advice column letters and answers. Discuss them a bit—most students will be familiar with the concept. Then, give your student a copy of a letter (not the same one from the introduction).

Version 1:

Both the teacher and the student receive the same letter. Each person has 3-8 minutes (depending on the level) to come up with some advice (separately). The teacher and student share their advice to see if it's the same or different and then have a short discussion about it.

Version 2:

The teacher and student each receive a different letter. As above, each person is given time to read and think of some advice. You can begin the discussion time by having each person quickly summarize the problem you have read about, then give some advice and discuss that.

Teaching Tip:

If you are familiar with local celebrities popular with your student, you can use current gossip to spice up the lesson. If X pop star has just had a public breakup, write a letter from that person asking for help getting back together, finding a new boyfriend, etc. For the men, a rumor of a football star being traded works well to get advice on how to improve that player's game.

Procedure:

1. Show some level-appropriate advice column letters. Read them together and discuss.

Version 1:

1. The teacher and the student get the same letter (not one from the introduction).

2. Each person has to read the letter and come up with some advice (separately).

3. Discuss each person's advice.

Version 2:

1. The teacher and student get different letters.

2. Give some time to read the letter and come up with some advice.

3. The teacher and student discuss the problems and their advice.

Board Games

Skills: Reading/Speaking

Time: 15-20 minutes

Level: Beginner to Advanced

Materials: Board game sheet, marker for each person (a coin or eraser)

Board games often come in the "teacher's resource book" that goes along with your textbook. If this is the case, you're in luck because you'll have a solid activity that your student will probably love with no preparation required. However, don't worry if there isn't a pre-made game in the textbook because it's easier than you might think to make your own. It will only take 5-10 minutes once you get a bit of experience doing it.

Use questions based on the grammar and/or vocabulary that you've been teaching during the previous lessons. Have some fun squares, such as, "Switch positions with the other player," "Rocks-Scissors-Paper. Winner moves ahead 2. Loser goes back 2," or "Go back 5 spaces." The style I typically use is a question of some kind where the person has to speak one or two sentences in response to it. You can use dice, two coins (2 heads = 5, 1 head + 1 tail = 3, 2 tails = 1), or a number sheet where students close their eyes and move their pen to choose a number.

Teaching Tips:

Board games have their own lexical set. It may be the first time your student has ever played a board game in English so it's useful to do some pre-teaching. Before you play, you can teach them some key phrases (it's your turn, go ahead, your roll, pass the dice, etc.).

Procedure:

1. Prepare the "game board" as well as dice or coins. Each player will need a "token."
2. Do rock-scissor-paper to see who goes first. The first person uses the dice or coins to find the number of spaces he/she will move ahead. That person answers the question or performs the action.
3. The next person rolls the dice and answers a question and so on.
4. The game continues until someone reaches the final square on the game.

Boggle

Skills: Writing/Reading

Time: 5 minutes

Level: Intermediate to Advanced

Materials: "Boggle" grid on the whiteboard/paper

You've probably played the word game Boggle before. You shake up the letters and then you have a certain amount of time to make some words with connecting letters. You can play it with your student without the actual Boggle game by making up a 6x6 grid on the whiteboard, or piece of paper. Then, you and the student have to make as many words as possible that are 4+ letters. You can give a bonus for longer words if you like. At the end, each person counts up how many points he/she has. You can double check for any errors. A way to make it fair when the teacher plays against the student is for you to only find words of 6+ letters while allowing the student words with 4-5 letters.

Procedure:

1. Prepare a "Boggle" grid or use the actual game (better!).

2. Try to make as many words as possible with 4+ letters. You cannot use the same letter in a single square twice within a single word.

3. Add up points.

o	r	p	t	s	a
e	a	i	e	t	f
b	k	n	e	r	i
a	d	r	g	o	r
c	o	t	l	s	e
k	f	h	m	a	n

Some possible words from this board:

green, pink, rake, back, fire, fires, fast, road, rose, fort, baker, sorts, steep

Brochure Scanning

Skills: Reading/Speaking

Time: 10 minutes

Level: Beginner to Low-Intermediate

Materials: Brochure/Timetable

Scanning is reading for specific information. Language learners tend to focus on trying to understand every word, so they need to practice quickly finding specific key words. This will increase their reading speed in general and help move them towards more natural reading practices. To provide realistic practice, collect travel brochures, bus timetables and menus. If you do not have local access to any of these, a quick Google search will give you a wide variety. Here are a few sample scenarios you can use depending on the level of your student.

Intermediate

Find a vacation bargain. Give your student a budget, length of travel, and any other limitations, such as "type" holiday (beach, historical, adventure, etc.). This is highly variable according to the materials you have available and your student's level. The student should scan the brochure for trips that match the criteria. To add more speaking, begin by discussing the student's idea of a great vacation, and then work together to find a trip that matches those criteria.

High Beginner

Try a new restaurant. Have your student find menu items with certain qualities, such as vegetarian, lamb, or no onions. Can he/she make a reservation for 8PM on Monday? What is the phone number for reservations? And so on.

Beginner

Take a bus from point A to point B for a meeting at a given time and then return. Have the student use a bus timetable to plan the journey. Have your student quickly scan the brochure to find the requested information. You can either have the questions printed in advance, or you can ask him/her to find certain information.

Any Level:

As a pre-reading activity, reproduce several paragraphs from a novel and give your student 2-3 basic questions to answer such as:

Who is this about?

What are they doing?

What color is the character's hair?

What is the character wearing?

Teaching Tips:

If your student is lower level, have printed questions for him or her to use with the brochure. For example, "What time is the last bus to _____ on Sunday nights?"

If you are looking online for printable realia, add "PDF" to your search and the results will begin with PDF files that match your search terms.

If you can get a Flight Centre or Thomson brochure, you can a lot of mileage out of it beyond scanning. They are basically magazines with hundreds of travel packages of all types and for a range of budgets, although nothing is too luxurious. The higher your student's level, the more freedom you have to expand the activity.

This can also be used with traditional texts as a test prep activity.

Procedure:

1. In advance, get a brochure or print one from the Internet. Restaurant menus, bus timetables and travel brochures are perfect for this. See the examples above for some ideas.

2. Prepare some questions for the student to answer using the information in the brochure.

3. Explain to the student that he/she is not to read word for word. He/she should only be reading to find the answers to the questions.

4. Have him/her find the answers to the questions.

Chapter Response

Skills: Speaking/Writing

Time: 10-15 minutes

Level: Beginner to Advanced

Materials: None

Optional Materials: Printed list of questions

Chapter endings make handy stopping points to check your student's comprehension and build a bit of interest to keep up motivation for the next chapter. These questions can be answered orally as part of a book discussion or written in a reader response journal and then discussed in class.

Some questions you can ask include:

What surprised you in this chapter?

What feelings did you have as you read? What made you feel this way?

What words, phrases, or situations in the chapter would like to have explained to you?

Would you recommend this novel to someone else? Why or why not?

How do the events in this story so far relate to your life?

Which character do you most relate to? In what way?

Which character most reminds you of someone in your life? In what way?

What do you hope to learn about (a character) as you continue reading?

What do you think will happen next?

What questions do you have that you hope will be answered in the next chapter?

Procedure:

1. In advance, prepare a printed list of questions about the chapter.

2. Discuss together in class, or have the student write his/her answers for homework and you can discuss them in the next class.

Character Problems and Solutions

Skills: Speaking/Writing

Time: 10-15 minutes

Level: Beginner to Advanced

Materials: None

This is a post-reading activity to include in a novel study or use with a short story. Choose a problem a character faced in the story. Discuss the problem and how the character solved it. Then, have your student brainstorm other ways the problem could have been dealt with. This is a sneaky grammar lesson. You can teach modals of regret (could/should/would have done/etc.) without getting too personal with your student.

Teaching Tip:

If your student is lower level, you may want to begin with a complete grammar lesson with scaffolded practice, such as worksheets, for the student to get some more focused practice.

Procedure:

1. Choose a problem a character faced in the story.

2. Discuss the problem and how the character solved it.

3. Have your student brainstorm other ways the problem could have been dealt with.

Conversation Starters

Skills: Speaking/Listening

Time: 5 minutes

Level: High-Beginner to Advanced

Materials: Conversation starters

These are 10 conversation starters that are guaranteed to get your student talking. You can use one of these questions as a quick warm-up to begin each lesson.

If I Won the Lottery

Discuss what you would do or buy if you won the lottery. I usually specify an amount of $1,000,000.

Bucket List

Think of five things you want to do before you die.

Guilty Pleasures

Explain to your student what a guilty pleasure is–they may not know. Then, it's time for confessions!

Things You've Learned Lately

Think of two or three things that you couldn't do as a child but can do now. Emphasize that it's related to a skill of some kind or you'll just get answers like drinking or smoking.

Last Purchase

Talk about the last thing you bought that was more than $100.

You're the President

Talk about what your top three priorities would be if you were in office.

Favorite Things

The student and the teacher each think of three questions starting with, "What is your favorite _____?" Then, it's time to answer them.

Horoscopes

Find some daily or monthly horoscopes online. Read their descriptions and see if they match.

People in Your Life

Who are the three people that you spend the most time with these days?

The Best Decision

Think of a difficult decision you made, of which you're confident you made the right choice.

Cosmo Quiz

Skills: Speaking/Listening/Reading

Time: 10-20 minutes

Level: Intermediate to Advanced

Materials: A Cosmo quiz or Cosmo-type quiz

If you are a guy, you may not be familiar with the quiz in each month's edition of *Cosmopolitan* magazine. These generally predict something about your relationship style, finances, etc. In other words, they are quiz-style horoscopes. They are pretty fun to do with your student because they are not meant to be taken seriously, but can tell you a little something about the quiz-taker.

Prep could not be easier: find a few old issues of Cosmo and copy the quizzes. Some of them are a bit risqué, so decide for yourself if you want to edit them a bit.

Begin with a brief discussion of personality quizzes: has your student ever taken one, etc. Give your student a copy of a quiz, read the questions, discuss the answers and keep track of answers in order to calculate the final "score" at the end. You can wrap up by talking about whether you and the student think these quizzes are accurate, fun or a waste of time.

Teaching Tips:

You can find quizzes at this website: www.cosmopolitan.com/content/quizzes/. However, the questions are given one at a time so your life will be a lot easier if you can get your hands on print quizzes.

If you think they are inappropriate for your student, you can make up a quiz in the same Cosmo style: ten multiple choice personality questions with points assigned to each answer. There are usually results for three point ranges.

Procedure:

1. In advance, prepare a quiz from Cosmo. You may need to edit the questions or leave some out.

2. Ask your student if he/she has ever taken a personality quiz and how he/she feels about them.

3. Together with your student, read the questions and discuss the answers, keeping track of the points to calculate the score at the end.

4. Finish by having a short discussion about whether these quizzes are useful, or a waste of time.

Deserted Island

Skills: Speaking/Listening

Time: 5-10 minutes

Level: High-Beginner to Advanced

Materials: None

Deserted Island is an excellent way to uncover what things are most important to your student. Tell the student that there is a terrible storm and his/her ship is sinking, but thankfully, he/she can bring three objects from the ship. It doesn't need to be realistic or necessary for survival, just something that they want to have during his/her time on the island. Encourage creativity and imagination. Then, discuss your answers together along with a reason why you chose each item.

Procedure:

1. Tell your student that the ship he/she is on is sinking. Thankfully, there is an island nearby that is already well-stocked with everything he/she will need for survival.

2. Each of you has to choose three things that you'd like to have with you during your time on the island. It doesn't need to be realistic or necessary for survival.

3. Discuss your answers together and why you chose each item.

Dictogloss

Skills: Speaking/Listening

Time: 10-15 minutes

Level: Intermediate to Advanced

Materials: A short story

This is a simple activity for higher-level students that helps them practice their listening and memory skills, and it's also good for substituting vocabulary words if the original word is no longer accessible. You can find a short, interesting story of some kind or make up one yourself. I've used various things: from children's stories to a story about something I did on the weekend. Just about anything can work.

Tell the story 1-3 times, depending on the student's level. You can also vary your speaking speed to make this activity easier or harder. Once you are done telling the story, the student will have to recreate the story that you told. It won't be exactly the same but he/she has to try to keep the meaning the same. Finally, tell the original story again so the student can see how he/she did.

This activity works well as a writing activity too.

Procedure:

1. Prepare a short story that you'll read to your student.

2. Read the story to your student 1-3 times, depending on the level.

3. The student attempts to recreate the story (speaking or writing), keeping the meaning the same.

4. Read the story one final time for the student to compare to his/her own.

English Central

Skills: Listening/Speaking

Time: 10-15 minutes

Level: Beginner to Advanced

Materials Required: Internet connection

English Central (www.englishcentral.com/videos) is YouTube for language learners. There is premium content and functionality, but you can enjoy many features for free. YouTube, of course, has subtitles on some videos, but English Central takes it to the next level. First, the videos are intended for use with students, so they have been curated and organized by level, topic and/or language skill. Each video is segmented for easy replay of a chunk of speech. Students can also click on a single word to hear it pronounced slowly and learn the definition.

Pronunciation is one activity you can use English Central for with your students. Have the student listen to a clip and repeat. You can pause after each phrase or sentence and repeat as needed.

Begin by playing the entire clip once or twice. Then, replay the clip, bit by bit, for the student to repeat. Each clip is a short story, so you can also watch and discuss and/or summarize as a 120-90-60 fluency activity (page 8).

Teaching Tips:

You can sign in with Facebook, but it would be better to set up a free account in your student's name or have him/her sign in with his/her own Facebook account.

If the student has difficulty with a particular word, you can click on that word and it will be played in isolation. If the student has trouble with a sound, rather than a word, there is a pronunciation section that focuses on phonemes.

Procedure:

1. In advance, make sure you will have an Internet connection.
2. Either select a video in advance or let your student choose one. There are "courses" that are sets of related videos, that you can work through in a series.
3. Play the clip once or twice first so the student can hear the entire thing.
4. Play one segment (sentence or phrase) at a time and have the student repeat, trying to copy the pronunciation.
5. End by watching the entire clip one more time and discussing and/or summarizing.

Find the Reference

Skills: Reading

Time: 10+ minutes

Level: Beginner to Intermediate

Materials: Newspaper article, pen

This is a noticing activity. In newspaper writing, care is taken to avoid repetitive use of the subject's name. This is the opposite of most ESL material, which makes frequent use of repetition to reinforce language. Your student will read a newspaper article and circle all references to the subject in order to practice recognizing the subject even when various terms are used to reference it. For a completed example of this activity, please see:

www.eslspeaking.org/reference.

Teaching Tip:

Use an actual newspaper, rather than a source such as Breaking News English (www.breakingnewsenglish.com), which may alter the text to reduce the use of varied referents.

Procedure:

1. Choose an article from a newspaper that has multiple references to the subject but uses a number of different referents such as, "Jones," "he," "him," "the 39-year-old," "the painter," "the father of two," etc.

2. Have the student read and circle each reference to the subject.

Flyer Time

Skills: Speaking/Listening

Time: 10+ minutes

Level: Beginner to Intermediate

Materials: Prepared flyers/ads and questions

This activity is used to practice answering questions with a visual aid. While your student is unlikely to be asked which bands are playing at X festival, he/she may need to answer questions about a presentation or report in English. In advance, prepare several event flyers or ads and questions. Prepare some questions that have the answers clearly stated:

"What time will _____ begin?"

"Where will this take place?"

Also include some questions that require the student to think about the event and use existing knowledge:

"Who do you think will be attending this event?"

"Will attendees need to do anything in advance?" (For example, make a reservation or buy tickets)

In class, give the flyer to your student and ask him/her to use it to answer your questions. Explain that not all of the answers are stated explicitly.

Teaching Tip:

The questions should mostly be content questions with a few purpose questions. The more advanced your student is, the more questions you should ask that are not explicitly answered.

Procedure:

1. In advance, prepare several event flyers and questions (see above for examples) for your student to answer using the flyers.

2. Let your student know that not all questions are explicitly answered on the flyer.

3. Have your student use the flyer to answer the questions.

4. Ask the questions. Do not let your student read the answers word for word.

Fortunately, Unfortunately/Luckily, Unluckily

Skills: Speaking/Listening

Time: 5 minutes

Level: Intermediate to Advanced

Materials: None

You may have played this game at school yourself. Start off by telling the student some bad news (something that "happened to you") followed by some good news. For example, "Unfortunately, my car wouldn't start this morning. Fortunately, my neighbor gave me a ride to school. Unfortunately, she drove through a red light. Fortunately . . ." Then, start a new cycle with the student, taking turns adding good and bad news.

Procedure:

1. Start a scenario (something that "happened to you") and do the first turn.

2. The student adds the next line and the activity continues, alternating back and forth.

If I Had a Million Dollars

Skills: Listening/Speaking

Time: 10+ minutes

Level: High-Beginner to Advanced

Materials: None

Optional Materials: If I Had a Million Dollars song.

This is an activity you can use to discuss hypothetical situations and to focus on conditionals. If you wish, you can start by playing the Barenaked Ladies song or video of the same name. Then, tell the student that there is a big Lotto drawing coming up, and you have a ticket and are thinking about what you'll do if you win. Give him/her several ideas of what you would do with a million dollars. Then, have the student share some ideas and discuss them together.

If you want to challenge your advanced-level students, find the song lyrics and cut and paste them into a worksheet, but omit some of the vocabulary words. Instruct your student to fill in the blanks while listening to the song. I find that one out of every 15 words is a good rule of thumb.

Procedure:

1. (Optional) Play the Barenaked Ladies song. I used a *YouTube* version with lyrics. Optionally, have the student fill in a worksheet with some of the song lyric words omitted.

2. Set up the scenario for your student: a big Lotto drawing is coming up and you have a ticket. Give the student several ideas of what you would do if you won.

3. Discuss your ideas together, including what the student would do with the money together.

Infographic Presentation

Skills: Reading/Speaking/Writing

Time: 1+ hour

Level: High-Beginner to Advanced

Materials: Internet access, PowerPoint

Optional Materials: Video camera

Presentations are a regular feature of ESL classes, but your student may get overwhelmed at the thought of first creating and then presenting a full-length speech. Infographics have become a common way of presenting information, and your student can create and use one to provide the "meat" of an informative oral presentation. This will also provide an opportunity to research a topic in English. If your student works in an office, he or she is likely to use PowerPoint at work, so the combination of something familiar (PPT) with something new (English presentation) should reduce stress.

Have your student choose a topic of interest to them that has several data points. For example, if he/she has a favorite team, he/she can find the team's current ranking, average points per game, number of championships, and so on to populate the infographic. The student should begin the project by researching several data points and finding an image or two online to use for decoration.

To create the infographic, the student will need to reset the margins to create the long, narrow look of an infographic. This is done by choosing a blank layout and changing the slide from landscape to portrait then adjusting the margins. Start with 10"/25cm by 30"/75cm and adjust if necessary. Your student can use images, Smart Art, and/or charts to present the data he/she will report. However, you may want to give your student a time limit for choosing a layout or have him/her make a sketch before opening PowerPoint, because the number of options can become a time waster.

Once the layout has been chosen, your student will need to fill in the data. If he/she is using charts, Excel will automatically to fill them in. Don't worry, it's pretty self-explanatory and the end result is right there for the student to see while working. Once the images are all in place, the student should add a brief explanation of each image. All images and text boxes can be resized, and the entire slide can be resized by adjusting the margins, if there is more (or less) information than expected.

When the student is satisfied with the infographic, it can be saved as a JPEG. This will probably have taken an entire lesson, so the presentation will be in the next lesson. You should tailor the focus of the presentation to your student's level and needs. A lower-level student may just need practice speaking without a script. Higher-level students may need to practice the use of gestures or inflection.

For the presentation of the infographic, pull up the saved image and have the student sit or stand next to the computer to present the data to you. A lower-level student may do best seated next to you with both of you looking at the screen. Being able to look at the image (and not having you looking directly at your student) should reduce quite a bit of stress. After doing several presentation activities, the student's confidence will hopefully increase and he/she won't need such modifications.

Teaching Tips:

If your student does not use PowerPoint at work and is not familiar with it (or if you do not want to spend an entire lesson making an infographic), you may want to have the student find an existing infographic online to present.

A video of the presentation can be helpful for your student. When students see and hear themselves, they can more easily see the areas that need improvement.

Procedure:

1. Have your student choose a topic of interest that would have several data points to research and present.

2. Have the student make a sketch of the planned infographic.

3. Using PowerPoint, have the student make the infographic (use a blank layout, in portrait, with the margins set to 10"/25cm by 30"/75cm).

4. In the next lesson, have the student present the infographic to you. According to the student's level, have him/her focus on speaking without a script, using gestures, or inflection, etc.

5. Review the presentation.

Is that Sentence Correct?

Skills: Listening/Speaking/Writing

Time: 10-20 minutes

Level: Beginner to Advanced

Materials: Blank paper, vocabulary words

This is a sneaky way to get your student to make grammatically correct sentences using the target vocabulary. Start off by giving your student 5-6 vocabulary words. They should be words that the student is quite familiar with already. The challenge in this activity is not the actual word; it's using it in a sentence. Give the student five minutes to make some sentences using those words (one sentence per word). Do not offer any assistance or correct any errors. You can also make some sentences using the same (or different, but familiar to the student) vocabulary words. Some of them should be correct while some of them should be incorrect.

The student reads his/her first sentence. Discuss whether it is correct or incorrect and why. Read your first sentence and have a brief discussion about whether it is correct or incorrect. The activity continues until all the sentences are done.

Procedure:

1. Give the student a few vocabulary words (and, as the teacher, you can use the same words or different words that the student is familiar with).

2. Instruct the student to write one sentence per word while you do the same with your words. Make some sentences correct and some incorrect.

3. Take turns reading sentences and discussing whether they are correct or incorrect.

Just a Minute

Skills: Speaking

Time: 5-10 minutes

Level: Beginner to Advanced

Materials: Whiteboard, timer

This is a very simple activity that you can use as a fast warm-up at the beginning of class in order to get your student talking. Write a bunch of general categories on slips of paper and put them in an envelope. The student must choose a topic at random and then give a short talk about it for a certain length of time depending on the student's level (beginner = 30 seconds, intermediate = 1 minute, advanced = 2 minutes).

Procedure:

1. Prepare general topics in advance.

2. Have the student randomly choose a topic and then talk about that topic for a minute without stopping. The goal is to have minimal pauses and not stop talking within the allotted time frame. You can increase or descrease the length of time depending on the student's level.

Teaching Tip:
Just a Minute is an excellent way to begin each class and you only have to do the preparation once. Continue using the same envelope with topics in it, but remove the ones that you've used to keep things interesting.

Just Fill in This Form, Please

Skills: Writing/Speaking/Listening

Time: 5-20 minutes

Level: High-Beginner to Intermediate

Materials: Application form

Filling in forms is an often-overlooked skill for language learners, but life is full of forms. To prepare for this activity, talk to your student in advance to find out what kinds of forms he or she has to fill out in English. Some possibilities include customs and immigration forms when traveling, banking documents, registration paperwork (such as for a doctor or a credit card) and job applications. Whatever your student needs, a quick Google search should turn up a generic example you can use in class.

Most forms have a fair bit of overlap in terms of requested information, so your student should get a quick boost of confidence, but there may be important differences in how dates and addresses are written compared to his/her first language. Any such variations can be quickly learned, and you can move along to the more challenging sections. The challenges to your student will be in the areas of vocabulary used on forms as well as writing responses in the way expected by those who collect the forms.

You can do this as a writing activity, discussing each section with your student, or you can complete the forms as a role play. For the role play, make two copies of the blank form so that you can each take turns playing the "information collector" and the "subject."

Procedure:

1. In advance, find out what kinds of forms your student needs to fill out in English

2. Find examples online and print two copies of each form you want to use.

3. With your student, take turns playing the part of the "information collector" and the "subject."

Mystery Case Files

Skills: Reading/Speaking

Time: Several hours

Level: High-Beginner to Advanced

Materials: Computer/ game-playing device, Mystery Case File game

Mystery Case Files are hidden object games with a mystery story available from www.bigfish.com. They are reasonably priced, and you get several hours of game play from each one. If you have a student who is really into computer games but not so excited about English class, this is a good way to entice him/her into participating. To gather clues, players must locate items on the screen from a list. This obviously lends itself to noun vocabulary.

Once a given list has been successfully completed, players are given a new clue to help them solve the mystery. The language used is intended for native speakers, and that's where you come in. Have the student read the clue aloud (or listen to the clip), and then discuss any unfamiliar vocabulary and its meaning. If it is a listening clip, be prepared to repeat it yourself to assist the student's comprehension. You can add a writing element to the game by having your student keep a written record of the clues.

As more clues are uncovered, continue to discuss them and try to solve the mystery. At the end, there is a resolution. At this point, if your student did not correctly solve the mystery, you can go over the clues to see if the two of you could have solved it if you had paid attention to specific information or whether some vital pieces of the puzzle had been left out.

Teaching Tips:

There are websites like casualgameguides.com which give "walkthroughs" of Mystery Case File games. These walkthroughs give tips, hints and shortcuts for each game. These games have reading and listening activities built in and numerous opportunities for discussion. However, your student may not want to pay you for something they think they can do in their free time. In that case, if the student's language level is high enough, encourage him/her to play for homework and summarize the story for you.

These games are also available as iPad and iPhone apps. Some are free, but have in app purchases.

Procedure:

1. In advance, choose a game at bigfish.com or iTunes. Play the game yourself to familiarize yourself with it.

2. Your student is probably familiar with computer games, but he/she may not be familiar with hidden object games where players have to locate items from a list in order to advance in the game. Therefore, introduce the game to your student and the objective (to solve a mystery.)

3. If you want to build your student's vocabulary, you can have a game dictionary activity to keep track of the objects.

4. When you encounter a new clue, have the student read it to you or listen to it. If necessary, repeat it yourself to make it easier for the student to understand. In either case, summarize the clue (in simplified language, if necessary) and discuss.

5. Have your student keep track of the clues, so that he/she can recall the previous information as new clues appear. Discuss the clues as you go through the game and try to solve the mystery before the end.

6. If the student does not solve the mystery before the resolution, go through the clues with him/her to see if he/she could have solved it by paying attention to certain information, or if some vital pieces of the puzzle had been left out.

New Language Pile Up

Skills: All

Time: 5-10 minutes at the beginning and end of class

Level: Beginner to Advanced

Materials: Index cards, pen

One benefit of one-on-one lessons is that you can help your student create a personalized set of flashcards, rather than just an ongoing set of new vocabulary lists. Throughout each lesson, each time the student comes across an unfamiliar word or phrase, make note of it on a blank index card. Wrap lessons up by going through each card, explaining the word/ phrase and giving the student an example or two of use in context (beyond the one from the lesson).

For homework, have the student look the words up in the dictionary and make his/her own sentences so you can check for comprehension the following lesson. You can begin with a review of the previous terms before moving on to new material. If you want to take it to the next level, have the student email you the sentences, so you have your own record of which terms he/she is working on. This way you can prepare periodic lessons to focus on and recycle the Pile Up.

Procedure:

1. Bring a pen and blank index cards to each lesson (or have the student bring them.)

2. Throughout your lesson, when your student encounters new terms, record one on each card.

3. Conclude the lesson by reviewing each term and providing additional examples of usage.

4. Assign looking up each word and writing an original sentence for homework.

5. Begin each lesson by reviewing the previous week's words.

Proofreading/Editing

Skills: Writing
Time: 5-10 minutes
Level: High-Beginner to Advanced

Materials: Worksheet/white-board

To keep proper grammar usage fresh in your students' minds, they should practice frequently. This doesn't need to be a full grammar lesson; a quick warm-up activity can do the trick. You can give your student a variety of errors to correct: word choice, word order, punctuation, capitalization, etc. The student should write the sentences or passage correctly.

Teaching Tips:

Begin by asking your student a few review questions about whatever rules he/she is practicing. ("When do you use capital letters?" or "What is a run-on sentence? How can you fix it?")

Procedure:

1. In advance, prepare a worksheet. You could even take a previous workbook activity and reproduce it.
2. The sentences or passage should practice previously studied points of grammar by having errors of that sort: word choice, word order, punctuation, capitalization, etc.
3. Have the student correct the errors.

Real House Hunters

Skills: Reading/Speaking/Writing

Time: 1+ hour

Level: Intermediate to Advanced

Materials: YouTube clip of House Hunters

If you have never seen House Hunters or one of its many spin-offs, it is a show in which a couple looks at three houses before choosing the one they want. After seeing each house, they talk about the good and bad points of each house (size, repairs needed, location, nearby transportation, etc.) For this activity, your student will watch one of the videos and describe it: furniture, colors, condition (new, old, stylish. . .), and give an opinion about it.

You could then finished with a discussion about the student's own house, using a similar format to the House Hunter video. Optionally, you could have a student make a video tour of his/her own house.

Procedure:

1. Begin with a clip of House Hunters from YouTube.

2. Talk about the kinds of information and issues the house hunters discuss: size and style of the house, necessary repairs, location, etc.

3. Discuss how the student feels about his/her own house.

Real Life Role Play

Skills: Speaking/Listening

Time: 5-20 minutes

Level: Beginner to Advanced

Materials: Variable according to the role play

Depending on your student's individual needs, you can create real-life role plays to help practice situations he/she may encounter outside of class. If your student is preparing to study overseas, this could include school application interviews, school situations, and everyday situations like ordering food at McDonald's or talking to a shop clerk.

To execute this activity, choose a specific role play, such as asking a clerk for help finding a shirt in a shop. If possible, go to an actual shop and you play the role of the clerk. Prompt the student to ask you for help finding something (for example: a shirt). You could then ask questions to get more information about the shirt: size, color, style (tee, button down, polo, etc.). If your student will have an admission interview in English, do some research to get examples of questions and rehearse them together. If you are using a textbook, this could be an excellent extension activity or an alternative to the provided dialogues.

Teaching Tips:

Play dumb: ask your student questions for clarification—ask them to repeat themselves, etc. to replicate those aspects of real-life conversations.

Speaking on the phone is much harder than face-to-face, so if your student will be moving overseas, practice phone conversations using real phones (or at least back-to-back).

Procedure:

1. Identify a real-world communication need your student has.

2. Play the role of the person your student will be communicating with. For example, go to a shop and play the role of the clerk. Prompt the student to ask you for help finding a shirt. Ask questions to get more information about the shirt: size, color, style (tee, button down, polo, etc.).

3. If using a textbook and/or if your student has no real world communication needs, use the textbook as a springboard for more realistic role plays.

Scaffolded Reading Online

Skills: Reading/Speaking

Time: 10-15+ minutes

Level: Beginner to Intermediate

Materials: Internet connection, Chrome browser, Language Immersion browser extension

Language Immersion for Chrome is a really cool free extension that turns web pages into scaffolded reading texts. Once a page has loaded, a percentage of the body text is converted to the target language. The translated text is highlighted and is defined if clicked. The amount of text that is converted is set on a sliding scale according to the student's level—the higher the level, the more text is translated. This is a good way to tailor the text to your student's individual interests and level at the same time. In particular, low-level students may become overwhelmed by a block of all-English text. Having the same amount of English dispersed in a much longer text can reduce their stress.

To use Language Immersion for a reading activity, download the extension file and have your student choose a blog, newspaper, or other website in his/her native language. Have the student read the selected text (it should be something he/she can read in a few minutes) and then have the student summarize it for you. Ask the student questions about the first language portion of the text. Then, open the menu and slide the level up. Have him/her re-read and summarize again. Once again, open the menu and reset the level. Have the student read one more time and discuss.

Teaching Tips:

Although this can be used with all levels, I would use this with lower-level students. For more advanced students, I would simply suggest they use this tool in their own time.
On my browser, it is pinned to the right side of my tool bar. To activate it, click the icon to open a menu with a choice of target languages and a sliding scale of level. The higher the level you select, the more text will be converted.

Not all websites are compatible. For example, Facebook statuses will not translate. You can copy and paste a text into Word if you want to print it out for use offline, but the clickable function obviously won't work.

Procedure:

1. In advance, download the Language Immersion extension using the Google Chrome web browser.
2. Have your student choose a blog, newspaper or other website in his/her native language that is of interest.
3. Have the student read their selected text (it should be something he/she can read in a few minutes), and then have him/her summarize it for you.
4. Ask questions about the first language portion of the text.
5. Open the menu and slide the level up.
6. Have the student re-read the text and summarize it for you again.
7. Repeat one more time.

Sentence Substitution Ladder

Skills: Speaking/Listening/Writing (optional)

Time: 5-20 minutes

Level: High-Beginner to Low-Intermediate

Materials: Sentences

This is a simple activity to get students to think about how they can use the words they know. They will be very familiar with substitution drills, but this goes one step further to get lower-level students comfortable with using the language a bit more creatively. They have the knowledge, but they may need a push to use it.

Give the student a sentence practicing familiar categories of words (places, activities, etc.) and a familiar grammatical structure. Then, instruct him/her to change one word at a time to make a new sentence. Each position must be changed one time (as in, first word, second word, etc.), but it doesn't have to be done in order. Optionally, you can have the student write the new sentences.

An example ladder would be:

Original sentence: I saw a black cat walk under a ladder.

I saw an orange cat walk under a ladder.

We saw an orange cat walk under a ladder.

We saw an orange cat run under a ladder.

We saw an orange cat run under the bed.

We saw an orange cat run to the bed.

We heard an orange cat run to the bed.

We heard an orange dog run to the bed.

Teaching Tip:

Unless you want to specifically target articles and numbers, you can consider noun phrases as a single unit.

Procedure:

1. In advance, prepare several sentences using familiar categories of words (places, activities, etc.) and a familiar grammatical structure.
2. Have the student change one word at a time to make a new sentence.

3. Each position must be changed one time (as in, first word, second word, etc.), but it doesn't have to be done in order.

Story Timeline

Skills: Reading/Speaking/Writing

Time: 10-15 minutes

Level: Beginner to Advanced

Materials: None

Optional Materials: Sentence strips of important events in a novel

Extensive reading is an excellent way to build your student's vocabulary quickly, but you and your student probably don't want to spend too much class time reading novels. What you can do is assign a novel for homework and in each lesson, go over unfamiliar vocabulary or situations as well as any number of extension activities. This is one such activity.

A timeline, or chronology, of important plot events is a useful way to have the student briefly summarize the story chapter by chapter. A timeline will help him/her keep track of the story while providing practice determining important events. With lower-level students, you may want to scaffold the activity by providing the sentences for the student to order.

Teaching Tips:

If you are providing sentence strips, you can add extra, unimportant plot events and have the student select only the important ones to order.

Penguin has six levels of graded readers that include simplified versions of popular novels and classics.

Procedure:

1. (Optional) In advance, prepare sentence strips describing important events in the plot.
2. Have the student either order the sentence strips you have provided or determine the events on his/her own. If you are not using sentence strips, you can have the student complete the activity orally or in writing.

Tell Me More

Skills: Speaking

Time: 5-20 minutes

Level: High Beginner to Intermediate

Materials: Topic prompts, phone/ voice recorder

    This is a test preparation activity for standardized speaking tests. The TOEIC requires test takers to speak on 11 questions for varying lengths of time, while the TOEFL has six questions. Sometimes, preparation time is given but other times it is not. One barrier for many students is that they simply cannot keep talking, even about a familiar topic. In this activity, you will give your student a prompt and record him/her speaking, so you can record how long he/she can speak and how much relevant detail he/she can give.

    Consider for example, the question, "How often do you read the newspaper?" If the answer given is, "Never," the student will get a minimum score because the answer is relevant (as in, he/she answered the question), but the student did not provide any detail. There are many ways this answer can be expanded:

"I never read the newspaper because I am too busy. Anyway, I can hear about important events on the radio as I drive to work."

"I never read the newspaper because I can find out all of the news online or by watching the news on TV."

"I never read the newspaper because I know if something interesting or important happens, I will read about it on Facebook."

    You can see two things have been accomplished in this example: a reason and a detail have been added to the answer. Obviously, the longer the time limit, the more detail(s) should be given.

    To do this activity, give your student a prompt and record their answer. This will give you the exact length of the student's response and you will be able to review the response to determine specific areas which need improvement. By frequently practicing, the student will become accustomed to the format of the response and can focus on the content of his/her answer.

Teaching Tip:

Use the materials available from the testing company for the relevant test for this activity.

Procedure:

1. In advance, prepare speaking prompts from the relevant test materials.

2. Have the student randomly choose a prompt and prepare an answer according to the test he/she is preparing for.

3. Record the answer.

4. Review the answer with the student for length and completeness of response.

5. Repeat this activity frequently, if your student has a test coming up.

Test Prep: Describing a Photo

Skills: Speaking

Time: 30-40 minutes

Level: Intermediate to Advanced

Materials: Prepared images and accompanying vocabulary, timer (phone, kitchen timer, etc.)

Optional Materials: Recording device

Some standardized tests of English ability have a speaking task that evaluates how well the test taker can describe a picture. The image may or may not be accompanied by vocabulary the test taker must use in his/her description. Therefore, for this activity you should prepare several images and vocabulary, such as a noun and a preposition or adverb.

Depending on the level of the student, you may want to begin with some useful language, such as:

at the top/ bottom

on the left/ right

in the corner/ middle

"I think/ It looks like _____ (is happening.)"

After you have gone over the useful phrases, show the student a picture and ask him/her what is happening. Set the timer according to the time on the test the student is preparing to take (most are one minute). Encourage your student to describe it in as much detail as possible. Elicit further elaboration from the student, if necessary, until it becomes habit to keep talking for the entire allotted time.

"How is the weather?"

"What else do you see?"

"What do you think they are doing?"

"How do you think that person is feeling?"

Teaching Tips:

Remind your student to speak in present continuous when describing the image. ("The sun is shining. The man is looking at the woman as they walk across the beach. It looks like they are happy.")

If your student has a voice recorder or phone, record their responses. This will help track the student's progress as well as how long the student speaks each time.

You can extend the activity into general speaking by having a discussion related to one or more of the photos.

Procedure:

1. In advance, prepare several photos for your student to describe to you.
2. Review some useful phrases (see examples above).
3. Show a photo to your student and ask him/her to describe it to you.
4. As needed, encourage your student to continue describing the photo.

Test Prep: Reading Aloud Fluently

Skills: Speaking/Reading

Time: 30-40 minutes

Level: Intermediate to Advanced

Materials: Prepared texts

Optional Materials: Recording device

Some standardized tests of English ability have a speaking task that evaluates how fluently the test taker can read a text aloud. To prepare your student for this, choose several short passages for him/her to read aloud. During class, first model reading the passage aloud and then have your student read it to you several times. Give the student specific pointers after each reading. For example, if his/her intonation or stress needs improvement, mark the text to show which syllables to stress or where the intonation should rise or fall. If your student has a voice recorder or phone, record your reading as well as his/her final one for review and practice before your next lesson.

Teaching Tip:

I like to use www.breakingnewsenglish.com for this activity because there are a number of activities for each story, so you can easily build an entire lesson around one or two passages.

Procedure:

1. In advance, prepare several short passages for your student to read aloud to you.
2. First, model reading the passage aloud, then have your student read it to you several times.
3. Give your student specific pointers after each reading.
4. If your student has a voice recorder or phone, record your reading as well as his/her final one for them to review and practice before your next lesson.

Test Prep Speaking Activity: 5Ws and H

Skills: Speaking

Time: 30-40 minutes

Level: Intermediate to Advanced

Materials: Prepared speaking prompts, timer (phone, kitchen timer, etc.)

Optional Materials: Recording device

The speaking part of a standardized test of English ability has some similarities with the written essay portion: the test taker is asked to speak with minimal or no preparation time about a topic for a specified length of time. However, speaking tests have other elements as well. For example, some tests have speaking prompts focusing on personal experiences. Some common prompts include:

Describe a person who has had a great influence on you.

What is your happiest childhood memory? Why?

Describe a place you like to visit.

To get full marks, test takers need to give a full answer. To do this, have your student think like a journalist: 5Ws and H. To use the above example prompt of an influential person, your student should tell who the person is and how the person influenced him/her. Your student should elaborate by including when and where they met. He/She can emphasize how long they have known each other, why the person was influential, and what specific qualities the person has that impressed the student.

When you think your student is ready, provide a prompt and set the timer to give him/her one minute to prepare. When the timer goes off, reset the timer for two minutes and instruct your student to begin speaking. You may want to record your student's answer for the two of you to review and to track his/her progress.

Procedure:

1. In advance, prepare several speaking prompts for your student to answer.

2. You may want to have an example prompt to model for your student fully answering a question.

3. Whether you model the activity or not, point out that the student will need to expand the answer to fill the time. Keeping the 5W and H questions in mind will help him/her remember to include a variety of details.

4. Give the student a prompt and set the timer for one minute to allow him/her to prepare a response.

5. When the timer goes off, reset it for two minutes and have the student begin speaking.

6. You may want to record the response if the student has a voice recorder or phone.

Test Prep: Speaking to Essay Writing

Skills: Writing/Speaking

Time: 40-60 minutes

Level: Intermediate to Advanced

Materials: Prepared writing prompts, timer (phone, kitchen timer, etc.)

If your student is planning to take a standardized test of English ability, he/she will need to prepare for the timed essay. The essay intimidates many students, but as long as they practice the expected format with the main categories of prompts (choose a side, explain or describe, and compare advantages and disadvantages), they don't need to be worried. One way to ease your student into essay writing is by using the prompt as a guided speaking activity to help him or her brainstorm and fully develop some ideas and opinions.

Once your student has a good idea on where he or she stands, he/she can put pen to paper. I also remind my students that there is no lie detector: if they have an opinion based on one strong reason, but the opposite opinion has numerous weaker reasons, then they should defend the easier position. You can start by introducing some important language such as linking words and phrases and opinion words and phrases.

Some examples of these are:

In my opinion,

On the other hand,

I think/ feel/ believe _____.

Some people think/ feel/ believe _____, but I disagree.

I'm convinced/ sure/ certain/ positive _____.

Some would say/ argue _____, but to me. . .

Once you have gone over these, give your student a prompt. Ask him/her to answer the question with one sentence. Then, ask why or ask for more detail. For an opinion prompt, try to get three or four reasons, and then have the student explain or give examples to back up those reasons. The more reasons the better because, once your student starts writing, he/she can focus on the ones that provide the best examples. Finally, ask about the opposing opinion. Why do some people have that opinion? For choose-a-side prompts, addressing the opposing position is a good topic for the third body paragraph.

Once the student has talked through the essay, it is time to write. Check the time limit for the test your student plans to take (but most are 30 minutes). Start the timer and let the student write. You can use the essay as the basis of the next lesson.

Procedure:

1. In advance, prepare a writing prompt of the style used in standardized tests (choose a side, explain or describe, and compare advantages and disadvantages) and a timer.

2. Start by introducing some important language such as linking words and phrases and opinion words and phrases. Some examples of these are listed above.

3. Give the student the prompt.

4. Instruct the student to answer the question with one sentence. Then, ask why or ask for more detail.

5. Once the student has given several reasons and examples, ask about the opposing opinion.

6. Start the timer and have the student write the essay within the allotted time.

7. Save the essay to use the next lesson.

Text Me!

Skills: Reading/Writing

Time: 15+ minutes

Level: Beginner to Intermediate

Materials: Paper and pens or two phones

    If you and your student need a break from speaking, have a text message lesson (or part of a lesson.) This activity is simple: pretend you are conducting the lesson from a distance. Write a task for your student and encourage him/her to write you any questions. Communicate via short notes while your student works.

    Of course, an obvious lesson you could have is texting in English. Texting is quite different from other forms of written English, so if your student is likely to need to communicate by text in English, introduce him/her to "text speak" (common abbreviations) as well as common emoticons as they are different from culture to culture.

Teaching Tip:

    You can provide subtle correction by demonstrating correct usage of any vocabulary or grammar that your student misuses.

Procedure:

1. Briefly write a task for your student to complete without speaking. Specifically request he/she asks you (in writing) any questions he/she has about the task while working.

2. Communicate back and forth in brief messages to one another.

Where Are They Now?

Skills: Speaking/Writing

Time: 10-15 minutes

Level: Beginner to Advanced

Materials: None

    This is a post-reading extension activity that can be done orally or in writing. When you finish a novel or story, have the student imagine the main character five or ten years in the future. Where are they? What are they doing? How have the events in the story affected his/her life?

Teaching Tip:

If your student has difficulty, help them with brainstorming. Show him/her how to make a mind map with items such as: relationship, job, hobbies, home, pet, etc. Talk with your student about how his or her own life has changed in the past five or ten years.

Procedure:

1. After reading a story or novel, discuss how the character changed over the course of the story and why.

2. Have your student write or discuss what he/she thinks the character's life is like five or ten years in the future.

Who do you Want at Your Party?

Skills: Speaking/Listening

Time: 5-15 minutes

Level: Intermediate to Advanced

Materials: None

This is an excellent speaking warm-up activity for higher-level students. Both the teacher and the student have to pick four famous people (dead or alive) they'd like to invite to their party. Then, they have to say the reason why they're inviting them. I do an example like this:

Person: Michael Jackson

Reason: He has a cool house with lots of toys and he can play some dance music for us.

Procedure:

1. The teacher and student each think of four famous people (dead or alive) that they'd like to invite to their party and why.

3. Share and discuss answers with your student.

Word of the Day

Skills: Writing

Time: 5 minutes

Level: Beginner to Advanced

Materials: Whiteboard/paper

You can easily start a Word of the Day activity for your student by giving him/her a single word each day from the textbook, current events or by having a theme for each month.

Give the student a handout with the definition, part of speech, and several example sentences. Include space for a few more example sentences that you can make together. Have your student keep these in a folder. Make sure you review these words periodically throughout your time together. A little quiz works well for this.

Variation (more advanced): Idiom of the Day is where you give the student an idiom with a definition and a picture (if possible). Have him/her make 1-3 sentences using it correctly.

Procedure:

1. In advance, prepare a collection of words from your student's textbook or another source.
2. Begin each day (or one day per week) with one new word. Introduce the word just as you would regular vocabulary: present the word, the definition, part of speech and several example sentences.
3. Have your student make a few new sentences with the word.
4. Add all or some Words of the Day to regular vocabulary quizzes.

Would You Rather

Skills: Speaking/Listening

Time: 5-10 minutes

Level: Beginner to Advanced

Materials: List of questions

"Would You Rather?" is a fun party game. You can buy ready-made decks, but they aren't ESL specific. I make my own cards, but you can just make a list of questions or do this without materials if you can think of choices on the spot. One example is "Would you rather have eyes like a fly, or eyes like a spider?" The student must choose one and explain why. You can also share your answer and have a short discussion about it.

Procedure:

In advance, prepare cards with two choices—the weirder, the better. For example: "Would you rather have eyes like a fly, or eyes like a spider?" If you want to do this without cards, simply give the student two choices and have a 1-2 minute discussion. The student can also ask you a question if he/she would like.

Before You Go

If you found 39 Awesome 1-1 ESL Activities: For Teenagers and Adults useful, please head on over to Amazon and leave a review. It will help other teachers like you find the book. Also be sure to check out our other books on Amazon at www.amazon.com/author/jackiebolen. There are plenty more ESL activities and games for children as well as adults.

Made in United States
Troutdale, OR
01/19/2024